Jar of Wings

by Becky Cheston
illustrated by Diane Greenseid

Harcourt

SCHOOL PUBLISHERS

Printed in China

ISBN-10: 0-15-350561-3
ISBN-13: 978-0-15-350561-4

Ordering Options
ISBN-10: 0-15-350335-1 (Grade 5 Below-Level Collection)
ISBN-13: 978-0-15-350335-1 (Grade 5 Below-Level Collection)
ISBN-10: 0-15-357562-X (package of 5)
ISBN-13: 978-0-15-357562-4 (package of 5)

11 12 13 14 15   0940   12 11 10

The moon rose high and full above the bush that Lewis called home. Tonight, he sat in a splash of moonlight on a long twig with his friend Jade. Together, they munched on berries while engaging in their favorite pastime: moth watching.

Suddenly, Lewis rose, wiggling his moss-green body in the air. "Look over there!" he called. A large, brown moth rose into the air. The two inchworms watched in awe. "Just think," Lewis whispered. "We could end up like that."

Jade sighed. "I can hardly wait."

3

As it turned out, Jade did not have to wait for
long. The next day, she began to feel slow and heavy.
When Lewis set off down the branch to feast on some
tasty leaves, Jade refused to follow.

"I don't know what's wrong with me," she yawned.
"I don't feel up to an excursion."

Lewis turned back. What he saw took his breath
away. "Jade—you're molting!"

Jade looked down along her body. Sure enough,
her outer layer of skin was shedding, peeling off in a
corkscrew shape. "It's happening!" Jade's voice was
positively gleeful. Finally, she was transforming from
caterpillar to *pupa*.

"Whoa—I can't do that," said Lewis. He watched as Jade spun threads of silk around her body.

"I didn't think I could either," shouted Jade. Soon, she was wound tight as a mummy.

"Bye, Jade," Lewis called out. "See you soon."

It wasn't long before Lewis began to feel like Jade had felt earlier. The sun was just going down when Lewis began to spin his cocoon. By morning, both inchworms were asleep inside their silken shells.

Two weeks later, Lewis woke to find
himself in total darkness. Where were the
stars and the cool night breeze?

He turned—or tried to. Something was
wrapped around him. Then Lewis remembered. He
had woken up in his cocoon. Underneath the silken
layer, he was wrapped in his precious new wings.
Lewis shook himself and felt the wings loosen. He
began to rip apart his cocoon. His wings hung limp
and folded by his sides. After a few quick shakes, they
stretched up and out, a splendid shade of brown.

Now, Lewis looked for Jade's cocoon. Gone. Maybe she'd emerged already and was off trying out her new wings. He was a bit disappointed that she hadn't waited for him. However, Lewis had an even bigger problem.

His branch, part of a large, full bush, looked much shorter. The branch had been snapped off! Also, where was the bush? It had to be somewhere nearby. Trying not to panic, Lewis flapped his new wings.

"No matter," he thought. "Now I can fly off and find my home in no time at all."

Lewis waved his wings and for a few giddy seconds, felt the joy of flight. Then—*whack*! He crashed straight into... air? He picked himself up. Something invisible blocked his way. Soon, Lewis discovered that the barrier was circular, penning him in on all sides.

"You won't get out that way."

Lewis turned. A furry brown face stared at him.

"What's the matter?" said the animal.

"Haven't you ever seen a hamster before?"

"I don't think so," said Lewis.

"That's glass you're in," said the hamster. "Get to
know it. Watch out for it. It's not entirely invisible, you
know. Look carefully, like so." The animal turned his
head to one side. "You can see reflections."

Lewis turned his head. The hamster was right.
Now, he could tell that the hamster was also shut in
glass—only his walls were straight and square.

"My name is Cookie," said the hamster, "and don't
laugh. The human named me. Her name is Bella—
and she's harmless. At least, she means no harm."

"I can't stay in here!" Lewis cried. He had just begun his life as a moth. Flying from bush to tree with his friends had long been the pinnacle of his hopes, the high point of his inchworm dreams. How could he live his life in a glass jar?

The conversation between Lewis and Cookie was interrupted by a loud, girlish voice. "Hi, Cookie—I'm home!" The next thing Lewis heard was Bella's squeal of delight. "Yes! You're out of your cocoon!" Bella tapped on the glass with one finger, sending turbulent sound waves booming through the jar. Lewis held himself very still, willing the girl to go away.

Later, while Cookie played on the floor with Bella, Lewis dozed. He woke in darkness—a moth's most active time. From his jar near the window, he could see the full moon high in the sky, a lone spotlight. Lewis fluttered to the edge of the jar. That's when he spotted Cookie, pressing his nose against the glass.

"How did you get out?" Lewis asked.

"I usually run around the room a couple of times a day—when Bella's at school or asleep." Cookie pointed to the girl, who lay snoring softly under a quilt. He explained to Lewis that he'd figured out long ago how to climb out of his cage.

"Really?" Lewis asked. "Why don't you get out of here?"

"I love it here!" said Cookie. "Why would I want to leave?"

"What are you doing out, then?" asked Lewis.

"Helping you, of course. You're not going to last long in that jar. Plus—a friend of yours has been banging against the screen all evening."

"A friend? Who?" Lewis asked.

"She calls herself Jade," said Cookie. "She went to hang around the porch light for a while." The hamster stole a look at Bella, who was mumbling in her sleep. "Let's do this quietly—and quickly."

Cookie scaled a pile of books and jumped onto the jar lid. Then he nibbled around one of the air holes until it seemed big enough for a small brown moth.

Finally, Lewis crawled out. "Wow," he said. With a few quick flaps, Lewis zoomed up to the ceiling.

"Take it easy," said Cookie. "This'll only take a minute." The hamster was already at work chewing a hole in the screen. "That should do it. You ready?"

Lewis flew down to join his friend Cookie on the windowsill. "Thanks, Cookie," he said. "I owe you one, my friend."

"Don't mention it," Cookie said. "As soon as you get out, you'll see the porch."

"I'll come back to visit at night when Bella's asleep," Lewis said.

"That would be nice," Cookie said. "I don't get to meet a moth every day."

After saying good-bye, Lewis flew away from the window. He was flying freely now! He saw a beautiful bronze moth circling a ceiling light.

"Jade? Is that you?" Lewis asked excitedly.

"Lewis!" Jade cried, flying to meet him. "I'm so happy to see you! I missed you!"

Now, in the brightness of the full moon, Lewis saw something else—a familiar leafy bush. He was finally-back home!

Think Critically

1. How is Cookie a good friend?

2. Why do you think Bella brought home the cocoon?

3. What words does the author use to describe the moon when Lewis wakes in the jar for the second time, at night? Explain whether or not you think the description is effective.

4. What was your favorite part of the story?

5. Which is your favorite character? Why?

 Social Studies

Moth Research With a classmate, make a list of questions about moths that you would like to have answered. Then use reference books or the Internet to answer your questions.

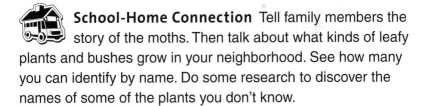 **School-Home Connection** Tell family members the story of the moths. Then talk about what kinds of leafy plants and bushes grow in your neighborhood. See how many you can identify by name. Do some research to discover the names of some of the plants you don't know.

Word Count: 1,149